THIRD SERIES

New Classics to Moderns

2

Contents

Yorktown Music Press

Published by
Wise Publications

Exclusive Distributors:
Hal Leonard
7777 West Bluemound Road
Milwaukee, WI 53213
Email: info@halleonard.com

Hal Leonard Europe Limited
42 Wigmore Street
Marylebone, London, W1U 2RN
Email: info@halleonardeurope.com

Hal Leonard Australia Pty. Ltd.
4 Lentara Court
Cheltenham, Victoria, 3192 Australia
Email: info@halleonard.com.au

Order No. YK22121
ISBN 978-1-78305-369-8

Edited by Sam Lung.
Music processing and layout by Camden Music Services.

Printed in the EU.

Air in D Minor

Z. T676

Henry Purcell
1659–1695

Le Petit-Rien

No.4 *from* 5 Pièces de Clavecin

François Couperin
1668–1733

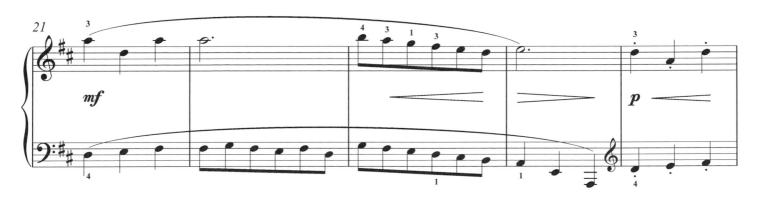

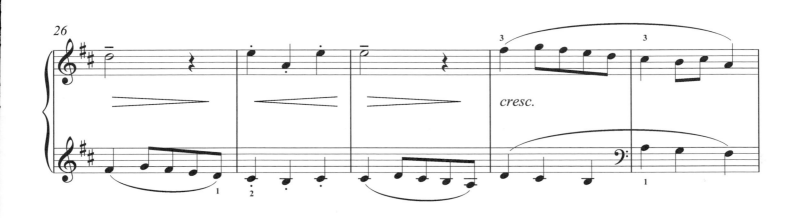

poco rit.

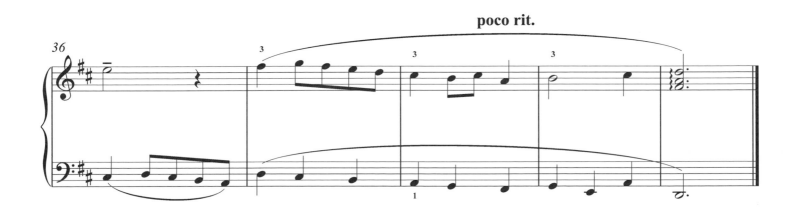

Bourée

from Suite in E Minor BWV 996

Johann Sebastian Bach
1685–1750

Minuet No.3

from 10 Minuets, Hob.IX:22

Joseph Haydn
1732–1809

Minuetto

Lesson 8 *from* Guida di musica, Op. 37

James Hook
1746–1827

Minuet, K.15c

No. 3 *from* The London Sketchbook

Wolfgang Amadeus Mozart
1756–1791

Andante moderato

Minuet, K.15pp

No.40 *from* The London Sketchbook

Wolfgang Amadeus Mozart
1756–1791

Miniature Rondo

No.22 *from* 120 Pieces For Aspiring Pianists

Daniel Gottlob Türk
1756–1813

Country Dance in D Minor, WoO.15

Ludwig van Beethoven
1770–1827

Ecossaise No.5

from Eight Ecossaises, D.977

Franz Schubert
1791–1828

Ecossaise No.8

from Eight Ecossaises, D.977

Franz Schubert
1791–1828

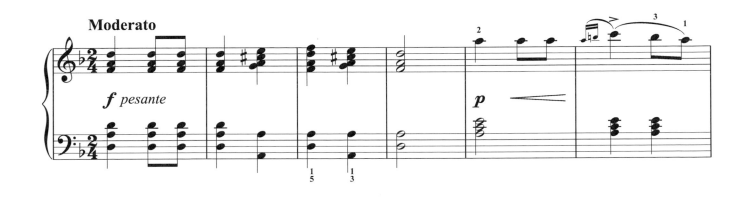

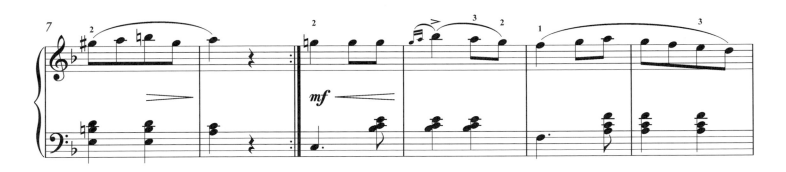

Melody

No. 1 *from* Album For The Young, Op.68

Robert Schumann
1810–1856

Song Without Words

Carl Reinecke
1824—1910

The Italian Pipers

Charles Gounod
1818–1894

To Begin With

No. 1 *from* Little Piano Pieces, Op. 81

Peter Nicolai von Wilm
1834–1911

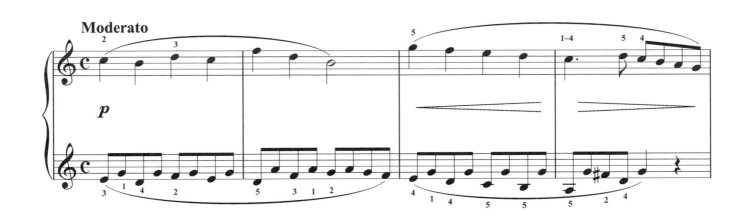

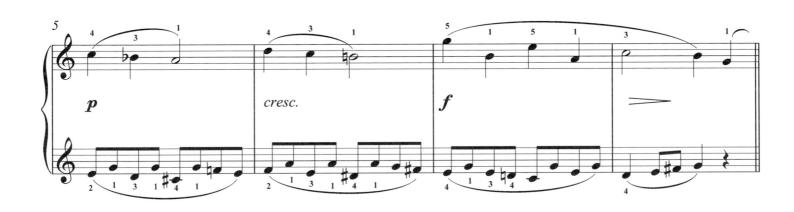

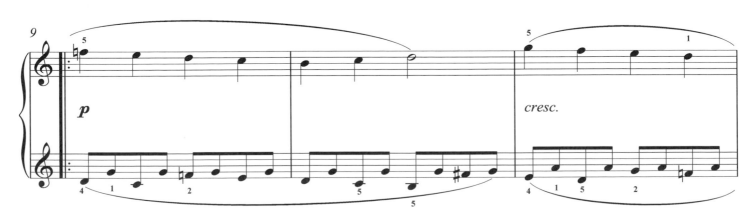

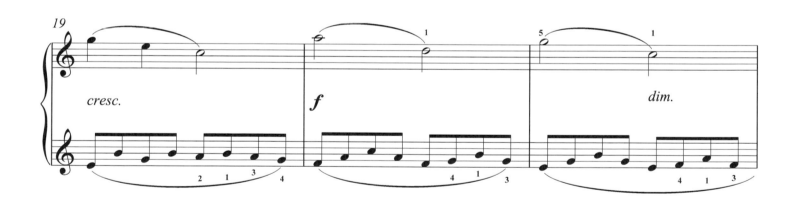

Piano Music For Young And Old
No. 2

Carl Nielsen
1865–1931

Andantino

No. 1 *from* Les Cinq Doigts

Igor Stravinsky
1882–1971

Prelude

No.4 *from* Five Miniature Preludes And Fugues

Alec Rowley
1892–1958

Triumphant

from Moods

Iain Kendell
1931—2001

The Swan

from Pieces For Angela

Kenneth Leighton
1929–1988

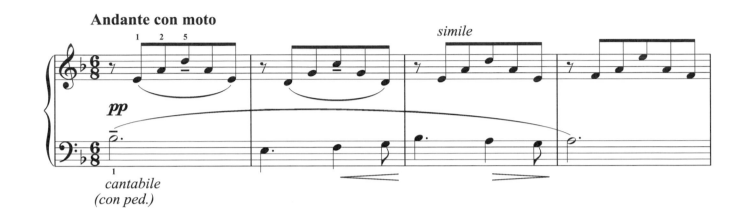

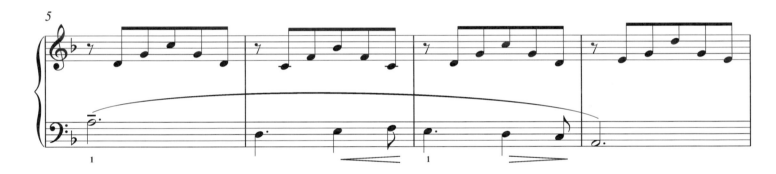

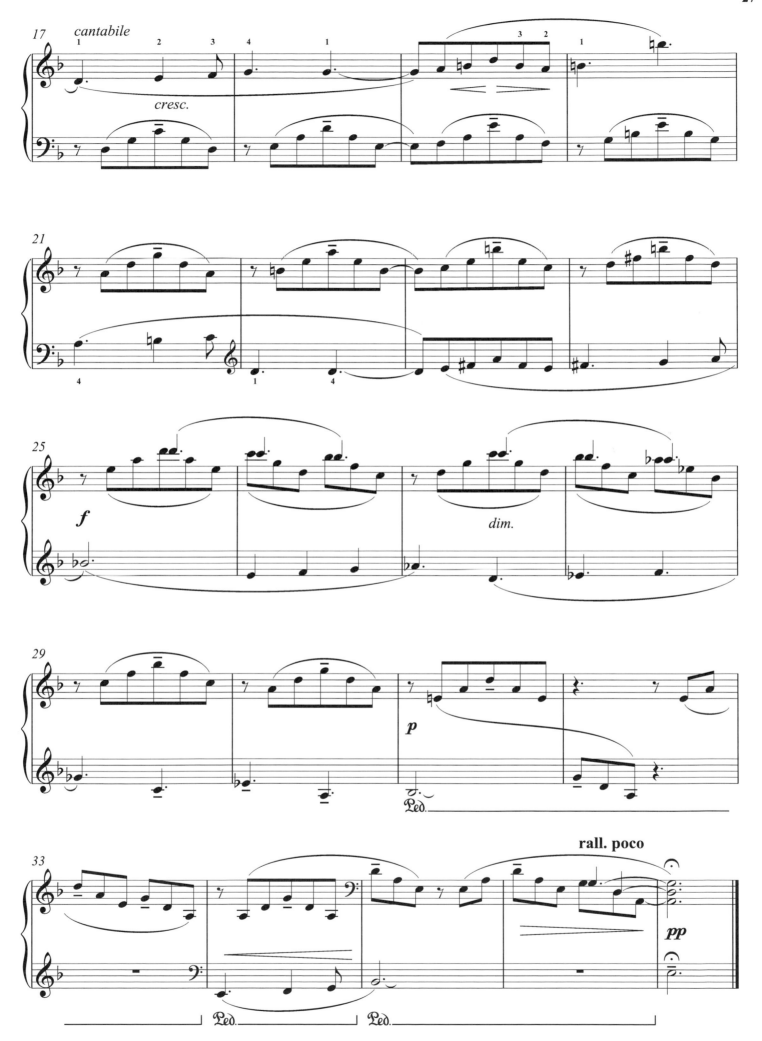

Six Secret Songs
No.2

Peter Maxwell Davies
b.1934

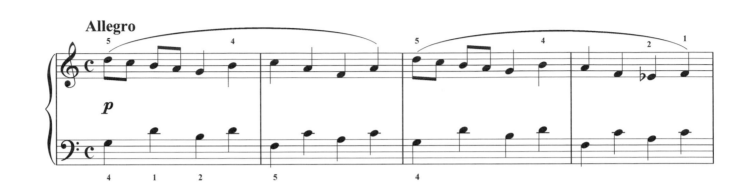

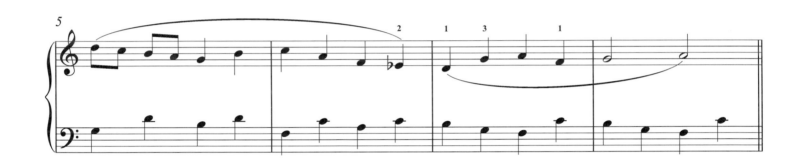

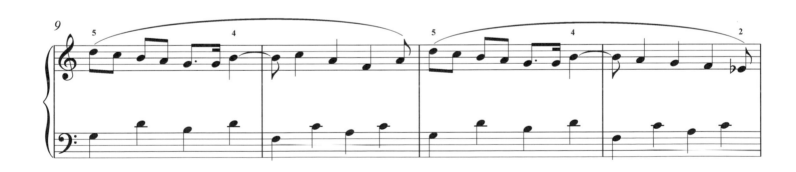

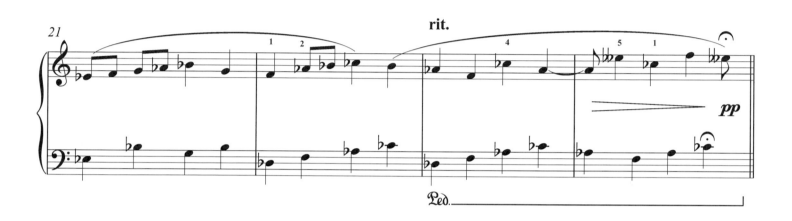

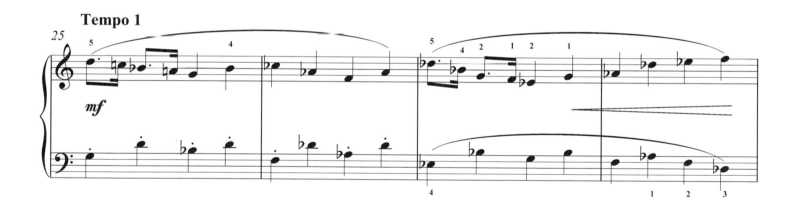

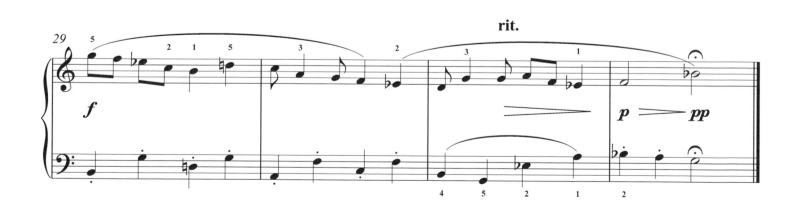

White On White

No.6 *from* Zebra Music

Giles Swayne
b.1946